REFLECTIONS AND PREOCCUPATIONS

REFLECTIONS
AND PREOCCUPATIONS

JAROSLAV HAVELKA

Published by Ergo Productions, P.O. Box 4460 London, Ontario, Canada, N5W 5J2.

Printed and bound by The Porcupine's Quill, Inc. (Erin) in August of 1980. The type is Syntax and the stock, Zephyr Antique Laid.

Photography by R. Bondy

Drawings by J. Havelka

Second Printing, February 1981.
Third Printing, September 1984.

ISBN 0-920516-05-X

Gratefully dedicated to all my students who have helped make my teaching meaningful and rewarding.

PREFACE

Every good teacher soon realizes that at the centre of every statement he or she utters, curled up and sleeping, there lies a question. Good students discover, rouse, and nourish those infant questions, and sometimes they grow so quickly that they pursue the teacher back to his office or follow him home, and linger in his mind for weeks, months, even years. An inspired teacher such as Jaroslav Havelka is not content to let the little creatures waste away in some outer waiting room (the easier strategy by far), but must get to know them as intimately as possible. In his case, those persistent questions become the stimuli for a book of meditations and aphorisms which can be offered back to the students who helped wake them up in the first place. The dialogue which results from genuine teaching never really stops.

I find that the most rewarding way to use *Reflections and Preoccupations* is as a kind of breviary for meditation. Find a pleasant, quiet spot, open to any page and ponder an entry for a few minutes. Calisthenics to keep the mind from getting flabby. And those sleeping questions can be aroused even in what sounds like an answer. Above all, this book encourages the activity of the mind. It implies that the curious, amazed mind is itself a definition of 'being alive'.

A possible added attraction for those who have listened to Jaroslav Havelka is that they may detect his particular idiom – the sonorous words, the cadence in phrasing, even a hint of a Czech accent. Best of all they will find the startling idea which catches the wind like a kite, trailing a long tail of metaphors. There is also the characteristic twinkle of irony in the midst of the serious. And the reader is always in good company. Dante, Shakespeare, Cervantes, Wordsworth, Eliot, Jung and Freud cavort together to the music of Mozart inside the cathedral-cranium of Havelka, who arranges and composes new music and dance steps from the choir loft.

Ideally, each entry should be read apart from the others and held to the sunlight like a fine jewel. Collectively, they form a constellation or a mosaic, held together at the centre by a core of recurring words and images. And that means they belong to their author alone, like his signature. Ponder, understand, hear, absorb, meaningful, wonder, silence, awe, revelation, unique, life, eternity. These recurring abstract words are part of the lexicon of philosophy and advice. It belongs to Havelka the teacher. The images in the metaphors which 'ground' that lexicon in experience belong to the poet and the painter: clouds, trees, leaves, birds, butterflies, sunlight, windows, angels, roses, and the underside of that list: stones, dogs, monkeys, ashes, shadows, and darkness. What we have in this book is a cohesive vision which can change its configuration like a kaleidoscope. Yet the pieces of coloured glass are always the same. The reflections often depend upon the angle of the viewer. For Jaroslav Havelka, however, it is all one large stained glass window to begin with.

It is also refreshing to read the work of a professional psychologist who treats the mind as more than a complicated set of sporadically firing neurons and synapses. The human mind depicted in this book is capable of reflecting itself back to itself like facing mirrors which reflect to infinity. Hence, one gets the impression, that the real business of the psychologist is to probe as deeply as possible into the processes of the mind (not just brain or intellect or memory alone), using not only empirical and clinical data, but even intuitive perception, metaphorical language, and the insights of philosophers and artists.

The result of this approach is the rich mixture of vocabularies that we find in these entries. We are given a whole garden of images complete with birds and clouds in the world above, together with Ego (the snake in the grass) and his antithesis, the Wise Man. Death and Fear are almost dismissed as minor characters. It is the creative synthesis of intellect, imagination and experience which makes this book such a wonder.

That is why I feel genuinely honoured to be given these pages to applaud, soundlessly but ceaselessly, this remarkable offering.

John Orange,
King's College,
London, Ontario.

CONSIDERATIONS

Commentaries on Experience

Living and Growing

Dimensions of Happiness

Teaching and Learning

Confronting the Self

Elements of Spirituality

Death as Beginning

Often I have a distinct feeling that I came to this life after spending more vibrant and significant moments in some remote past time. Thus my life's task appears to be rather simple, in that whatever I do and wherever I go, I should be looking for signs of that hidden, former glory. Yet only rarely do I detect some fragments of it.

Indeed, I wonder whether being really alive means seeking to complete that ancient broken mirror as much as possible.

□

The cosmos is a magnificent invitation to dance. We are the dancers. But we are doing exactly what is being done in the cosmic wholeness. So actually we are being danced.

No wonder that sometimes our heads reel and we experience vertigo.

□

It is dark outside. I want to look through the window into the darkness of night. Instead, I see my reflected image on the glass. Again my ego interferes.

To await something that has little chance of ever happening, is the mark of a wise and confident human heart.

□

Some eminent minds try to persuade us that Nature should be explained and demonstrated 'modo geometrico' — as essentially a network of straight lines, cubes, triangles, intersected points and perfect circles. Thus we become progressively a more circumscribed civilization of boxes, pentagons, hexagons, matrices, rectilinearity, projective geometry and topology.

What has happened to the curving branches, trembling of the leaves, drip of the mist, waves lapping at the shore, blobs of resin on the plum, and all the happily crooked and unstreamlined things under the sun?

Perhaps we are too easily bamboozled into a notion that the straighter, the squarer, the more clearcut, the more manageable is life, the better and more true it is. The corporate among us, the vivisective among us, the laser-loving and plumbing-admiring among us, the Skinnerian among us, seem to cherish this idea voraciously.

The birds, fish, flowers, rivers, trees, poets, and poetical loafers, true philosophers, children and sages disagree.

□

To be afraid of life is to be terrified of something within, something you insist upon as not being you.

□

In the twilight, a poplar is a needle stuck in the folds of a passing day's overcoat.

My right hand wants to write. My left hand is attentively helping, ministrating, not interfering, not trying to be important. My right hand tries to discover and formulate. My left hand listens carefully and obligingly to what the right one does. Which one do I prefer? I admire both of them. They are independent, differently effective and yet unified in a higher intention. I admire them both and like them for their quiet efficiency and lack of dramatic fuss. How much wiser they are than my silly ego.

□

When we speak, as it were, through a public-address system (and how often do we do that) we don't hear ourselves, and the others hear us as a bombastic fog-horn.

We even miss the opportunity to hear our friend gently whispering: *You are a fool.*

□

Somebody seems to be informing somebody else within me. Somebody seems to be constantly listening to somebody else within me. Of utmost importance to most of us is to which voice we pay more attention. The voice of the deep mind, or the voice of the ego? And yet only when we learn to listen to the unified voice of our whole being, do we listen properly.

□

To revere life is sometimes a prolonged cherishing of the deep silence between any sunset and any sunrise; sometimes it is a sudden understanding that our life endures in the wholeness like a stone in a plum.

□

Sometimes we are so greedy that we want to keep mountains and get rid of valleys; we want to inhale permanently and stop exhaling; we want to cage our life and sell it profitably to the best bidder.

Our two eyes, two ears, two nostrils and a mouth. Just seven small holes in the skull to receive images of the world. How can we ever hope to grasp the whole picture?

□

The Western images of man's condition and nature are essentially tragic.

Nature and man in it are products of creation, thus inferior and separated from the wholeness, subjected to a fall, disintegration and death. The realm of nature eventually ends in its destruction, and beyond its fragile limits there is an everlasting divine power, apart from it but controlling it. There is no other hope for man than through the redemptive will of God.

On the contrary, the Eastern images of man's condition and nature are essentially playful (lila), dancing and comic. All endings of nature or man are new beginnings in disguise. Regeneration is inherent in destruction. Death does not have dominion since it is only another act of play, a benign joke of a divine King.

The transitoriness of everything in this world is, for a Hindu, not a symptom of irreparable disintegration, but a sign of the self-renewing cycle of happenings which generates feelings of ultimate confidence that, in the end, nothing horrible and tragic can happen to us.

The comic element is born from an exhilarating sensation that the appearance (maya) of terror is simply a confusingly hilarious, illusory and incomplete story, the end of which comes about in a surprising and benign gesture of 'fear not'.

□

There is always somebody, somewhere, dancing and singing, and there is always somebody, somewhere, commenting on it.

I often miss someone. Is it my weakness or is it perhaps a natural human condition? Yet, when someone is regularly around me and close, my noticing him becomes habitual and thus progressively less meaningful. But when that person is absent, at once my awareness of him is awakened. Although this moment is often dark and worrying, the projected image of him is subtly sweet and, as it were, transcends reality. Then I start to miss him almost resentfully because of an intense feeling of incompleteness which is painful.

The ego is always incomplete by definition, and missing someone is a further painful reminder of that emptiness. The ego cannot miss with confidence and gentle absent-mindedness. But love can.

◻

There exists in man's mind a dim awareness that his Self — and not his ego — fulfills a magnificent task of realizing a unity between himself and the total universe. That is the exquisite work of the underlying intelligence of our mind.

◻

When confronted with something which threatens us, we feel at once insecure. We seek to escape from that into some compensating reassurance, into some illusory security outside ourselves. We grasp for any external support, are anxiously restless and tormented to the point of wishing for death.

We have failed to realize that insecurity is a necessary and constructive condition of our life.

We judge people mostly on what they say, somewhat naively expecting them to faithfully communicate their inner feelings and thoughts. That occurs very rarely.

Most of us speak first and think somewhat later. Only after a sentence is out do we rapidly notice its particular orientation and quality. We have committed ourselves through an expression and then our intellect forces the argument into a presumed agreement with the original statement.

Thus we are swiftly adjusting to what we have said, although the expression may only vaguely coincide with the inner feeling. We become the victims of our talking.

We don't know, seconds before we say something, what it is really going to be. We only follow a general drift or tendency of thought or feeling and look rapidly for a vehicle to take it across.

But after we have spoken, we have committed ourselves and must then defend the sentence, while actually ignoring its origin. Once openly committed, our intellect takes over, provides supporting material, arguments, further evidences, while the inner feeling has nothing to say and is usually ignored.

We are our own amazed, surprised and often embarrassed listeners.

□

There are rare mornings when, into the silence of pensive clouds, enters the sound of a distant wondering: you have been and never will be again. And yet you shall last like a crystal in the heart of a mountain.

□

We use our eye-blinks for self-defence – to interrupt a stream of overwhelming reality.

□

Most of our lives we imagine that the cause of our unhappiness is fear, anxiety, grief and death. Yet it is our incapacity to accept them that makes us unhappy and blind to the chances of a real self-actualization.

14

At times a motionless tree stands naked against an immense horizon. And at times we think that we are living.

□

Almost with a feeling of embarrassment I realize that if it were offered to me to live again, I would respectfully decline.

I wonder, is it a reasonable reaction? Surely life is not harsh to me, rather the opposite. And yet: No, thank you. Not any more.

Let me go deeper into it. I know that certain experiences would repeat themselves, but nothing really radically new would be added to my already established pattern of living. There would be the more or less known rhythms of disappointment and joy, of happiness and sorrow, of emptiness and elation. And the higher the peak, the deeper the valley. Is that all? There is surely something missing, but to gain that immensely important 'something', I would have to change into another constellation of being that waits for me on the other side, behind the door of death.

That reality, I know, I will not attain in this life, even if repeated. So, where does a wish to return originate? Maybe only in the fascination I have now with the mysteries of real life beyond.

□

The little sparrow on the branch is a part of life as we are. But he has a certain advantage over us. He is not forcing himself on life, does not argue with it or about it. He simply serves it in an awesome wave of faith and a joy of total acceptance.

□

If one man stands and another man sits, that may already mean that their destinies will never meet. Why not call it fragility of circumstances? If the sitting one stands up, it is a social confrontation. Why not call it a calamity of circumstances?

15

How admirable is the tree. I think particularly of its mastery over something as seemingly final as death. Look at it. Even if the green of the leaves is slowly disappearing, the tree continues its existence in a most powerful presence. A dry tree is still a structure of beauty. Its anatomy remains preserved. The same trunk, a cathedral of branching limbs, sublime curves and a unique stance. A witness of a majestic disregard for the sharp separation between so called Death and living organisms.

As well, the tree possesses a double cycle of growth. One cycle, similar to ordinary growing, that is from the stage of a seedling to an imposing old tree. The second, permeates and overlaps the first one, in which the tree remains subjected to yearly seasonal cycles. A cycle of greening, darkening, becoming red and yellow, shedding its leaves and donning a stern and silent nakedness of old age – to start a new cycle with a youthful greening again.

This amazing metamorphosis is completely missing in our life. In this respect we are closer to the impermanency of all things, and remote from a peculiar 'transcendence' of the tree. Thus the tree is more majestic and less tragic than human destiny.

□

Sometimes a warm thought possesses me. My friends grew from me like a rose from the earth and I am a mother to this friendship.

If they feel the same as I do, then we are two mothers caring for one child.

Biological anomaly but a psychological reality.

□

Why are very rich people often so miserable? They know how to make money, but they don't know how to get rid of it and enjoy it.

They are most impractical and illusion-bound individuals.

How many of my days are thought to be fragmentary, disoriented and often even useless? Because I always want to achieve something. To become somebody I am not yet. Or to become better, which is by far the most difficult.

Thus I keep pressing all the time while the achievement is not noticed. Yet an immensely more subtle achievement is at hand, that of being aware of my mind as it is in activity and in silence. But my demanding becomes its own obstacle, and I am not even interested enough to know myself – outside of my continuous desiring and judging.

Eventually, since I am not achieving what I have hoped to achieve, I become disgruntled and worried. Thus I aim at another chance to assert myself, knowing somehow that it is going to be a new failure. This is one of the most chronic, vicious circles that marks my immaturity.

☐

Civilization is a prolonged and seemingly never-ending process of developing strategies for making man independently comfortable in nature, and thus isolated from it. Culture and spirituality attempt to stop and reverse this process. Inevitably they are viewed with suspicion by any 'civilized' society.

☐

It is snowing outside. I detect some subtle feeling of isolation and the distant sound of Mozart's Andante cantabile.

I used to watch a snowfall with joy. But then I was a trusting child without sorrow, guilt and sin.

Now a snowfall can assume an almost uncanny appearance. A white darkness. There is a fear in me of something recklessly powerful blotting out into a white immensity the never-returning kingdom of my mother's heart.

Slowly I feel covered by snow until all traces of what I lived and loved disappear in silence.

Our society does not encourage us to wake up; consequently we are a society of sleepers.

On the contrary, it punishes us for any attempt to awaken to a realization that what is objectively considered to be a concrete collective 'reality', is actually a 'dream-illusion'.

The punishment imposed upon us is that we are classified as either antisocial or insane.

☐

Our thought is linear, temporal, separating, inferential, one-dimensional and selective, while the reality of the world is non-linear, multidimensional, simultaneous, non-successive and eternal.

When our thought tries to grasp the whole of reality, it is like seeing the mountains through a key-hole, enjoying a symphony from its first bar only or emptying the ocean with a tin can.

☐

When monkeys are making a racket on the left side, dogs are making a racket on the right side, and my ego makes a racket in the middle, although I know it is a holy bedlam, I realize with certain amusement that it is part of my life as well.

☐

As long as you keep making cautious, sidelong glances at authority, you are safe. But your vision may be badly impaired in the process.

☐

Our main trouble is not the fact that life seeps through us as through a loosely woven basket, but that we think, in that seeping through, that our life is being wasted.

To conceive of life as only purposeful is to limit it and to make a futile attempt to restrict it to some specific level of our plans and personal strategies.

Life's only significance is not in its purposefulness but in its meaningfulness. Actually, and paradoxically, only when we have discovered that life is without any purpose, do we find it valid without limits and thus meaningful. Only in that sense, life is – an inexplicable mystery. Only in that sense, life is awesomely worthwhile to be lived and cherished.

Without its mysteriousness, it becomes merely a convenient or inconvenient commodity for various purposes, which is a total falsification and diminishment of it.

□

Modern man's most ardent desire is for security. To be secure, we are told, one has to feel 'protected' from disturbing and damaging influences originating outside. Thus a search for security is a search to be successfully isolated from all dangers.

Life in its totality, being the carrier of these dangers, is viewed with suspicion and hostility so that a desperate quest for security becomes an attempt to escape from life.

But escaping means isolation, loneliness and eventually more frustrated feelings of insecurity. Thus a never satisfied desire for security is precisely the same thing as a feeling of insecurity. This is probably the most vicious trap for the living.

□

A nightmare of failure permeates almost every one of our social actions and intentions. And even when we succeed, we dream of failure and scream of anxiety.

Dakota Indians, Hopi and Zuni would consider this preoccupation as a most significant symptom of our 'civilized' insanity.

Sundays possess a peculiar beauty. I have always liked them. On Sundays I used to be more around my mother. I cherished my childhood play, my dreams, my readings, my fantasies.

Sunday now brings an emphasis on something that makes life festive, warm, absorbed in itself and magic. If it rains, Sunday has a melancholy accent felt in the roots of poetry, and reverberating in the Gregorian chant. Its afternoons spell a mysterious vitality of some unknown realities beyond me. It induces a feeling of the free floating benediction of purified emotions. And I, somehow remote from everything, seem to be fixed in a strange immobility surrounded by a hiss of impermanency. A gentle and sometimes a slightly nostalgic complex of the buzzing fly on my life's window-pane.

□

Present time is actuality itself, a fresh here and now without frills and romantic expectations. It is concreteness incarnate. Briskly and matter-of-factly emerging and gone again, it does not give us much chance to ruminate and sift through futile alternatives.

Naturally, it is not easy to live in the bare present, attended only by our enlarged awareness. The present is not only totally vital, but also austere, unexpected and delicately unpretentious, and yet so uniquely true.

Yet, how seldom do we fully live it in our expectations or among the dead relics of the past.

□

Although we constantly criss-cross, run over and step on the sun's rays, the sun never bleeds to death. Moreover, the sun never begs for commiseration under our heavy and indifferent steps.

□

To be alone and fear it, is loneliness; to be alone and not to fear it, is aloneness.

In some other unknown time, you may again be born into a summer day, full of gentle wind, rustling grass and the murmur of bees.

In that thought you may discover one terror of life's incomprehensibility.

□

Foretaste of infinity: a sudden clear realization that we cannot reach any destination — since we have been already there from the beginning of time.

□

We all carry in ourselves a germ of Dostoyevsky's Raskolnikov: we want to be accused, found guilty and convicted — but not to be caught.

□

Only the present can bring about an instantaneous experience of joy. The real 'I' is only in the present; the past and the future is the work of the ego. One cannot love anyone or anything when the present is not felt, as one cannot love only in thoughts of past and projected love. Thoughts of love are only commentaries on love and not an experiencing of it. Only the present state of awareness can be fully loving and lovable.

□

The most humble things of this world never stop softly calling for understanding, while sister grass and brother wind, for a long time already aware of our hollowness, run away from us in a receding wave from time to eternity.

□

Like a solitary pigeon in a darkening cathedral, a man of sorrow listens to an awesome draught of sound passing by him on its way to the unknown, where it dies away — before he can start his melancholy song.

To detect maturing within oneself is to notice that the constant crowding of thoughts and feelings becomes less dense, less hectic. Traffic slows down, and eventually only one thought at a time presents itself. Instead of a depersonalized mob of tiresome visitors, one encounters thought that possesses character, beauty and meaning. From that moment on, there is a state of aloneness where one thought and the Self are in a vital dialogue of communion.

Such communion is the benediction of aloneness.

□

Man cannot control himself unless he accepts himself. But by accepting himself he gives up the control, since he agrees to follow his nature, the current of his life's river.

So actually, before he can change his course of action, he notices that the change is already occurring, and he is invited to swim in it – realizing that that is the most genuine control there is. Life is a self-regulatory feedback and the control is not an extra push, but an alertness to the change. Man who has resigned the control of his life, has gained a deeper insight into the transformation already happening in his life from the beginning.

More and more I am inclined to think that real friendship is possible only with a few people. With people we generally like, we share some degree of communality, but our friends startle us by responding so much closer to the nature of our own aspirations, tendencies and sensitivities. At such time we seem to detect in our friends expressions of mental energy akin to ours. Energy which we both have in common, and yet – which is not personally ours.

This energy is of the universe and we were not fully aware of it before. Friendship is a realization of that happening within us. It is a benign confirmation of the similarities of our inner minds.

Every real friend is a most significant messenger of our belonging to the same order of things – and for that we are deeply grateful and thus lovingly committed to him as a welcome representative of the wholeness of universal energies operating within us.

□

What only surrounds us now, will sometime absorb us.

□

To survive mentally we must concentrate on everything outside and inside us with a much greater vigour. But then the word 'concentrate' does not really apply here. The functional word is 'aware'. That is, not to be exclusively preoccupied but fully immersed in anything that happens. To honour objects and people by being more aware of them. To see, hear and feel their innermost nature, and thus to notice their unique loveliness. This may be the most difficult task – the real heart of the meditative process.

But can I really be that attentive to the marrow of everything? Am I mature enough for that? Am I true enough, as true as the leaf is to the tree? Am I simple enough? Am I loving enough? Yet the whole process is a serene responsibility and a new, previously unknown bliss without which my life is superficial and empty.

The rose. Such an incomparably coordinated effort to achieve a temporal perfection of grace, beauty and serenity. There must be at the source of nature a hierarchy of preferred perfections; one of which is undoubtedly the realm of stars, trees, flowers and birds; the other, that of human beings.

To live a meaningful life is not only to notice such a hierarchy of perfections, but to help to recreate it in new contexts and patterns.

□

Never will I feel more serious, than on that one long gone wintry afternoon, when I suddenly knew that *I am*. It was then that I smelled for the first time the fragrance of the freshly upturned earth, and heard the leaves whispering about something beyond me and beyond time.

□

To be subject to changes and to be gratefully aware of them is an essential and vital part of living meaningfully.

To wish to remain unchanging, centered in our gratifications, wishing for permanency, is to live and die in a painful and frustrating illusion. Maybe even the Faustian quest is ill-conceived.

□

From time to time I must stumble over myself, in order to feel alive. If I merely turn the stones of habit and duty, I become despondent and irritated.

Perhaps the simplest and the humblest prerequisite of our awakening is first to notice the roots of oneself, and only after that to care for how the branches curve.

□

Even during the high tide of our passing time, we still keep on arranging that elegant tie, which presents us formally to the indifferent world.

How easy and how difficult it is to listen to music. Easy listening is the superficial one, where, while still more or less attending to the main melodic line, one selects some catching fragments and uses them to colour some ordinary emotions. In that sense, music fulfills a secondary function in underlying another activity and thus becomes an atmosphere maker. One uses it as a background for working, conversation, reading, etc. That is not really *hearing* music but only half-listening to it; it becomes a subsidiary happening devoid of any serious significance.

The other kind is more difficult, the real hearing, which results in a complete absorption into a new reality. An absorption so total that any musical phrase is received as a completely unique experience without any accompaniment of ideas, thoughts and emotions.

Musical reality is totally different from our cognitive processes. In hearing music, one concentrates on a unique and immediate progression, developing and shaping a current that reveals a new reality of sound order, beyond any grasp of the thought process.

Furthermore, it evokes a variety of new feelings, quite different from usual emotions originating in the established perceptual organization of reality in the world around us. Music does not describe anything. It only intimates possibilities of a newly discovered sound reality that evokes a unique quality of feelings.

To hear music is to become aware of an expanding universe of felt meanings expressed by sound. Not to hear music in its essential nature is to betray its mysterious uniqueness.

□

A rare and exquisite psychological state of the totally mature person: choiceless awareness. It is essentially an act of our total intelligence becoming aware of the true Self, through an undistracted attention, and thus a precise and faithful experience of expanded reality. Such experience underlies spiritual clarity and the highest degree of human freedom.

Being resigned to certain aspects of life does not necessarily diminish one's fears, it only changes them.

In detachment, things are quite different. What previously used only to frighten us, seems now to fascinate us as well.

While resignation is basically defensive, detachment is a dignified and fearless part of maturing.

□

One cannot strive for silence, desire it and possess it. One simply becomes silent. Silence stands outside the boundaries of what is me and what is not me. It is an absolute envelope encompassing more than the quiet does. Silence is not made but created. Neither is it the absence of any sound and activity.

It is a wholeness of a new emergence, even when sound and activity are present. It is a radical ground, part of which we become when everything else is removed, allowing us to be silent.

Silent people are extraordinary communicators of a realm beyond anything utterable. Quiet people have only chosen to suspend, temporarily, communication through sound.

□

Practically every day we come to a turning point of some sort. As long as we are willing to begin to look in a slightly different direction, the turning point signals aliveness.

As long as we keep looking behind at every turning point, we reveal the fact that we have died before our time.

□

If we radically suspect all of our pleasures, satisfactions and desires, then we are lacking both humility and humanity. If we fail in these two, all our pleasures, satisfactions and desires are suspect.

If we are humble and humane, our pleasures and desires fail to bother us, since they are honest and friendly.

26

How many people are wise and who may judge their wisdom? What sort of qualities would most of us agree upon? Level-headed, undisturbed, down-to-earth, habitually positive in reaction, possessing an amount of common sense. Is that what we mostly value in people who lead us? People for whom we vote, whom we promote publicly, who eventually succeed mostly in social interaction? But is that wisdom at all? Ponder it.

The genuinely wise people are not favored by the majority. They very rarely attain public offices; they are usually recognized late in their life; they do not appear to be the natural winners, successful operators, shrewd tycoons. They are rarely the pillars of society.

Wise people are often painfully ill-fitting, peripheral in any routine action and participation, and sometimes not even very pleasant. They stare at you too much to make you comfortable. They are too frankly outspoken when the truth is at stake and surprisingly silent when their own well-being and prosperity is at stake. They seem to be somehow out of this world and yet so deeply rooted in it, that they appear to be the only legitimate natives on our globe.

They speak better about absent than about present people. They often talk an unusual 'new' language with fascinating inferences, conclusions and extensions of meaning. They hate to judge, but their admonishment is deeply stimulating. Their influence upon us is usually memorable but not immediately detectable.

They seem to care for many more things than the ordinary man does and yet they do it without ostentation.

Wise men come before others and leave before others. Although they always seem to be involved in something, they are not hasty and worrying. What should a wise man worry about?

The wisdom of a wise man is a great absorber and soother. Worries are for him merely a procession of clouds drifting beyond the periphery of his mental horizon; they are there to pass and, after all, none ever returned.

□

Silence impresses me by its solemn insistence on expressing itself. Loud people have usually not much to say because they are not speaking for silence, the real maker of meaning.

□

When a man reaches mature stature, so that one is compelled to hear him, even though one may disagree with him, only such a man can make us at the same time humble, proud and grateful. Or angry with ourselves.

□

The real burden of trouble is often put on you by those closest to you. The real elation is to bear that burden for their sake. Thus, be aware that this burden is determining your significance.

□

Our life can taste like ashes, any time we eat it without being hungry for it.

□

Real forgiveness falls from above through the darkness of our anger, and when it splashes on the surface of our souls, we know suddenly that we have received permission — to forgive ourselves.

□

Our childhood is an unfinished song of *Te Deum*. We return to complete it with the waning of our life.

Although we often agree that love is an expression of a deep compatibility and confirmation, as friendship is, there is something else in love that is absent in friendship.

Love is the sudden realization of a uniqueness in the other. One becomes strongly aware of experiencing a state of discovery of an as yet unknown reality in the presence of the beloved. Contrary to friendship, in love one feels privileged to stare at a beautifully strange landscape with which there is no comparison.

In friendship, one is using, as it were, the same eyeglasses to see harmonious uniformity. In love, one sees the newness of things and one is struck by this unrepeatable insight. Thus, while the emotion accompanying any friendship is a warm wave of sympathetic agreement, love's emotion is different. It is an overwhelming awareness of the depth of one's own soul stirred by grateful amazement. In one moment, the beloved has charged our heart with gratitude for a discovery of new dimensions in life of which we were unaware.

The most natural development of any love is to become eventually a unique friendship punctuated from time to time by a reappearance of the same insightful radiance that took place at the beginning. In it, the lovers preserve a mysterious 'secret' revelation to each other, and only to each other, of the presence of the inexpressibly unique.

□

'This day will never come again' is a thought almost never stated as a mere fact, but one that is surrounded by an aura of melancholy.

Yet concentrate on it in the following way: this day will not be repeated because a new one is already being shaped and will happen tomorrow. Notice that there is no trace of melancholy.

□

When the flower's petals fall off, what remains of the crown they have once wrought and held together?

Happiness is a quiet assent to the reality of boundless significance. Our mind informs our heart about this discovery and thus happiness is primarily cognitive and only later emotional.

One cannot essentially enjoy happiness because enjoyment signals the end of it. Happiness, like love, cannot be cultivated and no amount of will or determination will bring it about.

Happiness is a rare gift received in moments of our deepest penetration into a fully understood and illuminated reality of being. Only self-reflection can detect its presence outside the reach of our ego. Our ego is only an interpreter, translator and historian of our mind's happiness. We can comment on it, analyze it, rekindle its past memory but cannot re-evoke it. It comes spontaneously in rare moments, and when we try to arrest it or concentrate on it, it vanishes as the water through our fingers.

Happiness is a momentous contact with eternity. It is a home-coming for an awestruck and silenced soul.

30

A most chilling sense of wonder is found in the realization that once you knew what you don't know now; that once you loved what you don't love now; that once you were what you are not now — and that you had almost forgotten all those yesterdays.

Real love may be a sudden remembrance of a loving kindness which, when you die, will not be forgotten anymore.

□

Am I sad with the sadness of the universe? What a preposterous arrogance. Yet what fascinates me is that even if I dismiss my sadness as a self-induced reaction of my deprived ego, it persists and keeps spilling beyond me. It has some strange peculiarity of its own.

It is a more subdued, peaceful and gentle sadness — there at the roots of me, and I feel its mysterious presence in the same 'place' where I feel, at some other time, happiness or beauty.

□

To celebrate anything is an appropriate occasion to wonder about the inexhaustible meaningfulness of human life. A dancing leaf happily boasts of its belonging to its tree.

□

Only rarely can a person experience a total acceptance of life. But if that happens, he feels a union with something to which nothing can be opposed, thus a pure happiness. And although he can again be involved in a conflict with pain and adversity, he lives his life with a wholehearted abandon and gratitude born from the understanding that all things are fundamentally good.

□

To circumnavigate the world in imagination is both delightful folly and a courageous cosmic enterprise. Undoubtedly, no 'decent' society will ever pay us for this trip.

When I am unhappy, I am seldom good. When I am good, I am not always happy. When I am happy, I am always good.

☐

The destiny of everything is formed in the flow toward fullness.

☐

And yet silence is as humble as grass; as humble as something that always stands behind, does not beg and does not assert itself; as humble as something not offered for evidence, for confirmation, that refuses to be labelled, proved, analyzed and explained.
I wish such a silence endured after most of my lectures.

☐

Where has it gone, that radiant cloud of my childhood under which grew my awe of everything that was, and began the wonder of everything that is to be?

☐

When a bird alights on the stem of a flower which bends to the breaking point, two innocent virtues meet each other: confidence and humility.

☐

A rose-bud is not a child to the rose — but only its promise.

☐

A chrysalis will never be a butterfly, since when a butterfly *is,* the chrysalis *was,* hardened into an unchanging immobility of the past.

32

A beauty too superb and looming large can torment our soul. We cannot absorb it as we cannot absorb our own shadow. Our soul remains too open and the draught of eternity chills our heart.

□

We stand on tiptoe to foresee our 'bright future', and when it arrives, without delivering the expected goods, we stand on tiptoe to foresee our next 'bright future'....
Meanwhile our present, unlived life, is like a dusty city parking lot. Sad and lonely, as a thistle.

□

Wasting a day should not be taken lightly. We often seem to waste it on banalities. And yet think about it, ponder it and be aware that many of the so-called trivial happenings or things are not as ordinary and banal as they seem to be.
Let us stop feeling guilty, feeling that the day was wasted. After all, how can anything in the universe be wasted? Rejoice in the power of cosmic ecology: recycling is all.

□

Our inner division is as evident as the separation of our body and its shadow. Only a light radiating in the zenith over our heads eliminates our shadow, as well as our separation from the whole.

□

If a thought does not open like a morning flower, it is not a thought at all, but the hazy twilight of the sea bottom of our mind.

If our acceptance of life is half-hearted, the possibility of happiness remains hidden and undiscovered. We are, in Gunter Grass's expression, 'die Halb-starken', not fully capable of living. In a Freudian context, we suffer from character neurosis.

□

What about hope? In a way it is a concession and complaint that things are not as they should be. Hopefulness is never an awareness of what is. It is a trust in something that is not. To be in hope is to have trust in becoming and to ignore being. If I am not something and wish to overcome this deficiency of not being it – I start hoping, thus confirming that deficiency.

But a man of faith is fully aware of what radically is; paradoxically, he is a man without hope. He starts hoping only when his faith is lost. Hopeful man is too ego-oriented. The saint's strength is not in being hopeful, but rather in being faithful to a timeless presence of total being which has nothing to do with the future and thus hope. A suicide does not so much lose the last shred of hope, but actually finds himself absorbed in a totally illusory hope and he punishes himself for that weakness. If one hopes that he loves, he does not love enough at that moment because he is speaking from an agonizing not-being-in-love which he abhors and hopes to change.

Hope is a preoccupation in a time of emptiness and lack of faith.

□

As civilized beings, we are progressively more remote from any 'participation mystique' with nature, which is a relationship the primitive man has but of which he is not aware, because he has never been conscious of any separation from nature.

34

To be surprised at everything and to be grateful for the surprise is to have achieved the most accomplished sense of wonder at, and reverence for, life.

□

Is there a relationship between our joys and our sorrows? Do they depend upon each other, forming an inseparable figure-ground union? Is there in every present pleasure already some element of future disappointment?

Are we trying to enter our happiness through an alluring gate of high expectations? Once the pleasure-happiness is attained, do we strive to preserve it indefinitely? Are we willing to pay the price for each of our pleasures?

Do we deserve happiness when we strive for it? Is it possible that after having examined some of these questions, we may abstain from longing for happiness? Isn't it wiser to listen calmly and gratefully to a hidden oboe-player, now intoning a sad song, and then a gently joyful one?

□

The most radical process of mental rejuvenation is to devote oneself fully to the recovery of the childlike consciousness which precedes the emergence of our ego.

□

Joy is an unexpected answer to a question that I have never asked. When joy appears, one sunspot of evil has been erased.

The last joy is returning to a home I never really left.

□

Too often, in this life, we cling to what gratifies us or flatters us, disregarding the quiet small voice of our true Self which prompts us to stand aside, to remain uninvolved, to let go.

The tree is wise. It does not complain and object to its rootedness in the soil, but endlessly plays with a gentle movement of its branches and leaves, plays with an improbable possibility of a mysterious liberation.

This may be the wisest playfulness of any object faithfully and humbly abandoned to its own destiny. A tree in the wind reveals the superb beauty of a serene reconciliation with the awesome force and wisdom of life. How incapable we are of this radiant wisdom, thus how much more sad and lonely.

☐

This year I am not building a cathedral. Thus I have so much free time to watch a butterfly dancing on the tightening drum of a grape.

☐

The purest happiness thrives on an immense void, like an inflated balloon thrives on the air. Essentially, there is nothing to be happy about – just happiness.

☐

We fear the day differently than we fear the night, but the fear is there anyway, mainly because we have separated one from the other and thus we are fooling ourselves and reality. Yet the rose of night and the rose of morning have the same fragrance.

☐

Power can never guarantee peace and freedom. But it may do so when power is united with character. Then it is actually power no longer but a strength of tolerant innocence, with none of the elements of forceful self-justification.

Every time we listen to music and enjoy it, we are inadvertently cherishing impermanence. We do not demand that music stop and endure whenever we like it best. It cannot be done. The nature and spirit of it would vanish. In its progressive, non-returning flow we find the truest essence of melody and its poetic meaning: intimation of impermanence merging with eternity.

□

Ecstacy is a state of total mind going beyond the limits of our ordinary pleasure seeking. It is a rare way of listening to a sound marking the rhythm of all there is. A subtle response to inner vibrations accompanying our existence, while yet separated from the whole; and a joyous premonition that this vibration continues over the threshold of our death.

It is a gentle reminder that the pulsation of life should not harden into a tension totally adverse to spontaneous, free and wonderful living.

Ecstacy is a courageous thanksgiving for even one moment of understanding that we were first born only to live, and suddenly we recognize life's awesome beauty. In that sense, it is the highest act in a celebration of life.

□

Few people will take you seriously after you signal your decision to spend the rest of your life observing butterflies, clouds, stones, running rivers, laughing children, and the swallow's descriptive geometry in flight.

But only after such a decision will you be a singularly free and happy person.

□

Boredom is the luxury of a plebeian mind. It makes a virtue out of simmering comfortably on the back-burner of our self-sufficiency. Boredom resembles overgrown finger-nails that prevent the natural touching of reality.

When everything which concerns me now shall pass, and a distant silence shall permanently enter into my life, then I will have gained the right to be content. Life will loom large in its significance, profoundly good and without contradiction or polarity.

I wish to reach that stage while I can still communicate with people. Only then will I become a real teacher. Only then could I truly enrich other lives. To become at last a happy messenger of the unknown. To know at last what grace and love are, and how they can be given to the other without any self-interest.

□

The more we paint ourselves into an absurd corner, the more we proclaim that we know exactly what we are doing, and that our absurdity is wisdom.

And we are hopping mad that someone keeps silently drawing with his fingers in the sand.

A real teacher does not actually teach the students anything, but uses an intricate ritual of cajoling, promising and stimulating, to urge them to find for themselves the real meaning of understanding.

If he succeeds, he merrily drops the label 'teacher' and becomes to his young friends a co-celebrant of life.

Thus the sacred art of 'judo' is part of any meaningful education, where the 'ju' (gentle) and 'do' (way) of cooperation leads to the most significant understanding of life.

□

Why do we look at a running stream, listen to birds, smell a rose, watch trembling and whispering leaves? Why do we sit and look at the gently swaying flowers and high flying wild geese across the autumn sky?

Can anything be gained and explained by even a careful scrutiny of the endless reasons, causes and motives? Where is the meaning of the question itself? Can anything be accomplished by asking it, when we all realize that an infinite regression into possible causes is plentiful evidence that we will never get the answer?

These are essentially meta-questions, questions shot into a mysteriously expanding universe. In some distant future, perhaps, these questions will become affirmations of certain dispositions and states, and so, not questions at all.

□

Even if the branches of the pine tree do not believe in their independence, they persist in drawing on the sands their own crooked image.

□

The real answer to everything occurs when one silence recognizes itself in the embrace of another silence.

To add a brush stroke to the incomplete and evasive Teacher's portrait: he is a Don Quixote, a valiant man of honour and lofty ideals which he imagines himself called upon to protect against the whole insensitive world; he has his wits turned by inordinate study but remains nonetheless sane and profound in his poverty and loneliness; his integrity is manly and his kindness is childlike.

He is a Hamlet, a convex and concave mind, reflecting the void of human existence and fighting it desperately; a sceptical contemplator and a haunted believer.

He is a Faust, an intellectual, and symbol-maker; a relentless seeker and builder of transcendental models which imperil his emotions but allow him to commit himself to the unattainable and find peace in it.

He is a Don Juan, seductive, graceful and elegant; a victim of his own insatiable desire for love and admiration; a tragic actor, a pretender and yet deeply concerned about the intangible human ties from which he is often exempted.

There is in each good teacher a fragment of each of these.

The best teaching involves a masterful use of metaphor which invites a young mind to an understanding of reality that suddenly looms larger than before, larger than any categorical reality.

A strong metaphor is an illumination of meaning, however temporary. It encourages a sensitivity to capture reality in its most truthful radiance. A metaphor is devoted to the emergence of a deeper as yet unknown level of experience and it has, in the skillful hands of a mature teacher, an inspirational function which offers an expanded and enriched version of life.

□

The more learned we are, the more we construct worlds that do not yet exist. The more educated we are, the more we intimate imaginary worlds that never will exist.

This may lead, however, to a chronic avoidance of the issue of living.

□

Hamlet had yet something to learn: that to be or not to be is *not* the question. 'To be' is the most essential happening of the whole universe in its never-ending current of combinations and permutations. Once having taken us in its stream, the universe is not going to 'unstream' us but only send us unpredictably either up or downstream. There is no 'not to be', but only 'what-else' or 'how-else' to be.

Poor Hamlet was too much impressed by the hole-ridden skull of his old friend Yorick, missing entirely the point that the holes are only the first signs signaling the transition, but not the end.

How should we love children? Let us ponder.

Make them fearless through surrounding them, especially in the earlier stages, by 'removable' protections. Protect them and support them to the point where fear and pain become their personal problems. We cannot and should not try to solve their fears and anxieties. Thus we should lead them gently to learn how to look into any anxiety without avoiding or fighting it. The mature lesson is that anxiety grows in proportion to the attention given to it.

Teach them slowly the great art of aloneness. Show them a never-ending compassion and not an agitated worry which betrays our primary preoccupation with our own comfort and drive for gratification. A well-developed compassion means gentleness and a lessened impact of nervous emotions.

Above all, through a wise use of detachment, stop short to point out to them, rather insistently, that we love them. Yet we must be cautious; after all, we may not. Consider that. What we may really want is to succeed in them, attain a pleasure and satisfaction in them, enlarge our importance through them, be more often than not on the receiving end. That of course has little to do with loving.

Be deeply involved when children are in trouble, when there is little chance that they will give us pleasure and glory. If they give us moments of joy, let us notice sharply whether looming behind is our demanding and gratified ego; if so, then it was not happiness in the first place, but a self-congratulatory pleasure.

Try to notice only the meaningful in their existence: that they *are,* and that they are unique and thus precious, and for all that we are profoundly grateful, as every real lover is. Therein lies happiness for us. In that understanding is our love. Because love is first an understanding before it is an emotion.

If someone teaches you how to be reconciled with yourself, bow down to him in the old Russian fashion.

Either he is a sage and deserves your bow, or he is a clever rascal, and in bowing down, you won't see his phony face.

□

On receiving a harsh truth about himself, the enlightened man declines to judge and condemn himself. He knows that self-condemnation caters to the ego. By judging himself, his better part, as it were, condemns the nastier part of him and that in itself is a form of ego-elevation, a sort of inverted self-approval. An immature person needs an emotion of self-abasement in order to foment within himself other emotions, those of self-pity and anger, which he needs so much to keep on living. He becomes a total slave to his emotions.

Enlightened man notices keenly, observes detachedly, and shows in his subtle indifference a deep mistrust of his own ego and its emotional tricks. He, like a superior actor, does not dissolve in tears when performing a moving scene but seeks primarily to understand the feeling, the non-emotional aspect of his emotions. He notices this extended nature of his emotions with detachment, which only means that he grasps the greater depths in them.

He *understands* his emotion and thus is neither in conflict with it nor a victim of it.

□

If we are too preoccupied with the task of improving our lives, we may easily forget to live. By being too busy reading the train schedule, we may miss the train.

Not long ago, I lectured to an interesting quasi-religious group. Early spring and a beautiful old country-house. Cordial but somewhat solemnly embarrassed people. Not exactly simple but somehow honestly simplified like gently stained old barnwood. I spoke on 'Alienation in modern man'. At first I felt uneasy. I started in a low key (for me the shortest way to get to my ideas) and I think that I captured their attention.

Slowly they responded with a sincere and deep involvement. While this involvement seemed to preserve intellectual and logical crispness, it also welcomed a subtle contact with the glow of understanding which always surrounds any meaningfulness. It was a response of intelligence in its widest sense, a courage demanding freedom that can reach beyond any factual message. My words were only a pretext for that transformation. I was only an instrument while they became spontaneously alert to the movement of their own intelligence, active in a state of peculiar 'resonance'.

In that state, one becomes a 'carrier' of a message through a wider context of awareness; becomes attuned and committed to something 'out of the ordinary' and yet immensely ordinary, that reverberates in a new meaning. When this resonance happens, a shift occurs, as it were, to a new gear and one listens with a new, absorbing intensity. So did they. It was a strong experience and satisfaction for me, the unwitting instigator.

People without talent are usually consistent. You can rely on their mediocrity. They iron everything into flat orderliness and in the process burn holes in the fabric of life.

It does not necessarily mean that gifted people are inconsistent, but when they are too consistent, they become embarrassed like a dog who has leaked on the carpet and wishes that he'd never been born.

□

When we examine our students, surely we must think that the fragments of knowledge we have given to them are worthy of being remembered and repeated. This can be misleading. Knowledge is important in any real education, only when it leads to understanding; and understanding is not *about* reality but *of* reality. Now, how can we examine that?

□

Some universities are concrete reservoirs of talent, whose dam was unfortunately constructed up-stream. They dry up rapidly, and instead of being used for the irrigation of the fields of intelligence, they become a barren place for the military excercises of Ph.D. programmes.

□

Our educational system claims to prepare us for the future, and that is a semantic confusion. Any education worth a candle must prepare us for the present, since 'educare' means to lead out – from dependency on the past and from the uncertainty of the future.

To be educated means to be independently committed to the unique validity of the present. And that means to sail in the middle of the river of the vital energies of our present existence, seeing the shores on both sides retreating, while the river widens into a delta, and the delta merges with the sea.

45

Now there is time for me to think of aging, without remorse and sadness. To begin to listen to myself in the way a silent violin listens to the echo of a past sonata, which keeps reverberating even in the absence of the dancing fingers.

I see myself again standing barefoot and grateful under the endless sky with its unforgettable passing clouds. I do not ask anything anymore of my lovely youth, because now I am a collector of healing herbs, slowly disappearing into the mist of mysterious mountains.

I keep watching the gently swaying branches of my beloved trees which taught me the first lesson of wonder. Slowly I refuse to play with Death the game of hide-and-seek, for I have ceased to take too seriously that 'solemn Dark Lady' without humour and thus without substance.

I know more than ever that nothing ends, but everything changes and matures into a higher, unknown constellation of amazing truth. I am gratefully attuned to the subtle music of 'finale gracioso', which never signals the end, but burns larger and larger holes into the fabric of night, until light has full dominion and illuminates the unimaginable vastness of another life.

This is not a message, just a brief reminder from an aging teacher to his young friends, who are bound to age as well, to do it more gracefully and more humbly than he did.

□

There are moments when I feel like a useless servant, like an insignificant crust of milky moonlight on an abandoned meadow, a futile absorption of a shadow into the hardened purity of a frozen lake, over which passes a procession of humanity, without ever noticing my presence.

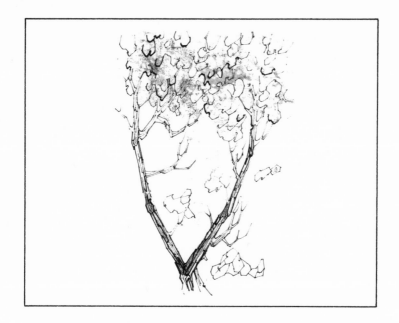

As strange as it first seems to be, in going deeper into myself, I soon realize that I am entering into a part of me much more expanded than my superficial ego. Into 'something' larger and subtler than the continuous and dusty record of my social conditioning, that record of reactions which I learned to identify and cherish as the most effective, concrete and desirable agent of my living.

This 'something' deeper in us finds some expression in its amazed and grateful openness to the total being, which in Eliot's phrase is 'the still point of the turning world'. It is a capacity to look creatively at reality with pointed directedness, so that we see it as it is, in its Suchness, without any ego-oriented admixtures of wishes, aversions, fears and prejudices. In general, that complex of feelings which habitually interferes with what we are looking at and should see – clearly and unclouded.

☐

Sometimes I am moved by the realization that I will never say what I was once about to say but never said.

How much adjustment is needed in my life? Adjustment to what? To the precisely organized system of 'yes' and 'no' of my society, leading me in a procession of basically small talk, responding in proper time to proper questions in proper order.

I am expected to adjust like a musical instrument out of tune, to a proper key in which the monotonous song of a social contract is being sung. I am being encouraged to keep pace, not to remain behind, not to press too hastily forward, just to affirm the necessity of the common call and the common march. My presence is actually mostly appreciated, not when I am singing alone, but when I am a member of a plainsong choir, whose voice merges with the others without any distinction. I am solemnly expected to join a laundered humanity that protects me in effacing me. No sharp edge, no chirp of private joy, just affirmatory self-negation.

Since my late childhood, I have had a deep dislike and aversion for this process of human adjustment which still keeps dehumanizing me. However, there is another process of affirmation immensely superior to any adjustment. It is a fundamental affirmation within each of us, a silent but urgent inner assent to a primordial 'yes' to what is not our own, but part of what we are. I don't have to model myself to it through a self-effacing social adjustment. No adjustment is necessary. Here an innermost reality is making itself felt as the most authentic actuality of my life. In it I am not promised any advantages, but through it I receive a tacit signalling, that I am, and in that I am most precious.

I affirm myself through my own roots that grow beyond me, but include me. In that moment of affirmation, I am offered infinite possibilities of commitment to this freedom, the only freedom there is.

A struggle for some strange supremacy goes on within me all the time. Supremacy of something I want to associate with in a fight against the inner enemy. There arises a tension and I am too well aware of it.

In a way, I am trying to escape from something from which there is no escape, and I know it. Sometimes in moments of contentedness an intensive hope begins, but that is already the start of a renewed impasse.

There remains a longing for something unknown, accompanied by a bitter feeling that it is not to be had. And this longing is vital and unsuppressible.

It is a longing to overcome and to be.

□

Even the mosquito, like us, never knows whether his buzzing is more true in the daylight or during the night.

□

Evening should not be 'spent' but lit into a glowing radiation. Rarely do we capture a fleeting reflection of it. Instead we hasten to 'spend' the evening and somehow succeed in strangling it.

Yet evening has a delicacy which is missing in the day. The day is primarily for the ego, while evening and night are for the Self.

□

There are two metaphysics of my soul: my dreams and my imagination. My dreams express in strange configurations what is basically inexpressible in words and thoughts; my imagination links together what is expressible in words and thoughts in a new, previously unknown way. Both are talking the language of mystery, and although I am the spokesman of that language – do I understand it?

Do we really desire the truth above all? Even to the point of being inconvenienced and hurt by it? Not really. Surely a disappointing answer. Although ideally we have capacities and dispositions to aspire to truth, practically our primary concern is *to be right* and not to be true.

Now, to be right is a 'truth' with self-serving modifications, tailored truth, conditional, truncated, a partial truth in the service of selfishness and self-justification; it accommodates our prejudices, biases, licences and idiosyncracies. And since no half-truth is true, to be right is not to be truthful but to be most actively engaged in a dialectic, in which we thrive so lustily: in order to prove that I am right, I must first prove that the other is wrong. My righteousness feeds on somebody's error.

We desperately need to prove our adversaries wrong and then our half-truth or untruth becomes fully justified. We feel just and virtuous because they are unjust and false. A justification of our righteousness through someone's wrongness breeds the most pestilent atmosphere that surrounds our personal and social life.

In that atmosphere we conduct our business, politics, education, committees and family life. And so when this ominous dialectic attains a boiling point of confrontation and conflict – we feel totally 'justified' in hating, fighting with any available violence and destroying with satisfaction.

Naturally, our justified aggressiveness offers to the enemy an additional reason to hate us even more and to wish to crush us. Thus, in the name of truth, but through the ugly practices of our unjust, blind, and hateful self-righteousness, we are ready to face any disaster or holocaust, and are even proud of it.

Ash Wednesday. What is another person to me? How distant that person is from me and I from him. Two remote stars fixed in their determined orbits and only rarely crossing their ray-paths.

Two solitudes imitating concern and pretending involvement, while distrusting the unknown solitude of the other. Sartrian 'les autres'. Sometimes they feel and proclaim love toward each other. But how do they do it, these self-centered, self-favoring, self-adulating ones? What do they really want from the others? Perhaps some hopeful expectation in further self-completion, which the other can presumably help to fill.

Only when the other can offer something that is missing in me, do I seem to be moved to like him, and absorb in myself what he has and I don't have yet. An awesome, never-ending piracy, expropriating, bartering, acquisitioning along with grim self-interest.

I cannot really mean it! It would be too harsh and ugly. Don't I know enough of human loving kindness and nobility? Of self-less loving and silent sacrifice? What is it that whines in me? Who laments? Which part of me is freezing and needs warmth?

Who is really afraid and hurting if the whole of me longs so strongly for them, my friendly 'enemies' and 'fearful' lovers?

□

The deeper I go into myself, the less I am in my own ego. To my surprise, my innermost happenings go on by themselves spontaneously like the passing of an autumn or the drifting of a cloud.

□

Before I was, how many times did I play in the sandbox behind the distant star?

From where did it rain on my bewildered eyes, dedicated from eternity to stare into the receding cosmic lights gently swaying under the breath of silence?

I am frightened of any form of sentimentality. Is it perhaps that I find it foreign to my own disposition? No. I fear it because it is a threat which originates within me.

Occasionally I follow an emotion to a point where it deteriorates into a self-laceration, ending in self-pity and sickly sweetened self-love. That is, indeed, a process of sentimentalization of any emotion. There I realize my ego's self-asserting reaction, which I detest in others to a level of disgust.

All my life I have struggled against certain emotions. Emotions that are susceptible to sentimental deterioration. The more I live the more I am aware that the richness of one's responses is determined by strong and yet subtle feelings, and not by inflated and overheated emotions. Feelings have their roots in the detached functioning of our total intelligence; emotions only in our egos.

I know that any sentimentalized emotional episode does not promote my maturation, but leads me astray into a bewildered defensiveness. Such deteriorated emotions blind my understanding and disturb a network of subtle responses. Unless I am able to transform some of my emotions into strong and yet serene feelings (containing always some element of detachment), I feel insecurity, turmoil and nagging anxiety.

Sentimentality weakens any approach to reality, cheapens it, confuses our vision of it and dominates us because it caters so strongly to our egotistic interests.

□

There are rare moments, when I cherish everything by giving up everything. Then the generous heap of life seems to be growing higher than the Himalayas.

One stands in front of me and I know he barely listens; he gets some of my words, but the emphasis and omission is his. He selects, picks up what he needs, and disregards the rest, often without me knowing about it. He listens selectively, but does not hear me.

And I? Rather a similar story. His answer interests me mostly to the degree it enhances my argument. I have no time to hear him fully, since I am primarily busy paying attention to my thoughts and not to his. A painful game of how one 'outlistens' the other.

When I really listen-hear, I absorb and remain silent. At that moment I have no time for anything else. To be a good listener-hearer is to get all that is being said and more through deepened involvement. To be just a successful listener is to get the bare stimulus that allows me to assert myself better. What a waste: so much noise and so little sound.

□

Only a higher order of complexity can comprehend something that is of a lower level of complexity. Thus we can never exhaustively know the working of our minds. To do so, we would have to be of a superior mental organization, or trans-human. In that sense, psychological investigation becomes the most frustrating and 'self-limiting' process.

□

As I was passing his sandbox, a little rascal asked his mother: 'Hey, Ma! What is he?'

I got lost quickly, not willing to hear his mother's reply.

□

Was it you who stood behind the broken window? And which desire was stronger in you — that it had never been broken, or that you had broken it yourself?

Last night I met a great, silent midnight, a dark cow with a collar of gently jingling stars around her neck ... and she ate the grass of my useless sorrow.

□

There is always 'something' that belongs to things and that is beyond our understanding. Just as mysterious as the sun's 'belonging' to the maturing strawberry.

□

We cannot force ourselves into self-reflection, but slowly and gently we can adopt it as a most significant ingredient of daily living. In this way we enter into a habit of capturing, dwelling upon and sifting through a number of remote fragments of consciousness.

Then alone consciousness becomes richer, fresher and extended beyond its own fringes. It is an invigorating and sometimes very demanding process that can grow on us and make us mentally livelier and more responsive to the fuller functioning of the mind. Without this self-reflection there is too much crowding of thoughts and feelings that pass the stage of our consciousness without much imprint. We are confusedly lost among the massive, often chaotic, sometimes excessively routinized functioning of our bewildered and yet hollow living.

Self-reflection makes our inner life vibrant, intensive, less sentimental, detached and more serenely curious.

□

My grandfather used to ask, 'Who shall say what is reality, and what is not?'

This question rings deeply and majestically, like a Welsh choir, through my bewildered brain many, many years later.

A rose drenched in gasoline will burn faster, but will lose its fragrance.

A plastic sunflower will survive the winter, but will not rejoice in the spring.

A man without loving kindness, vainly tries to remember whether he has ever lived.

☐

In the long run, the drama of our fight against presumed enemies, menaces and obstacles is less important than the intention of overcoming in order to be.

Often a dramatized life so highly acclaimed as truly real, and one which absorbs quanta of our energies, is only a deeper often unconscious desire for merging with the undisturbed realm of being.

Thus this asserting ourselves could actually be a strong, hidden drive aiming at the abandonment of all assertions, when we come at last to a vital contact with the universal within us, that does not know any conflict and contradiction.

☐

Our best friends are like cathedral windows. From the outside they may appear to be uninspiring, drab and ordinary. But from the inside, they are radiant, fascinatingly colourful and deeply comforting.

☐

Sometimes I hear somebody knocking on the door. But there is no one outside. It is my heart beating against all the imaginary walls of my time, space and consciousness.

It is my heart marking gently the rhythm of the universe.

The memory of yesterday strangely darkens our life in spite of the fact that we notice the past as something sweet, consoling and lovely. The fact remains that even if a memorable past contains a beauty, it also carries a shadow of being lost forever. Thus the past has always a double significance: it has a distinctly radiant quality of being permanent and unassailable, and yet it is steeped in the sadness of being no more. The sadness of unwanted transiency looms large in the memory of the past.

There is actually no sadness without involvement with our past, felt as a vanished moment of once known joy. And so, sadness of some of our past loves is but a chronicle, only a memory of past emotion, which we want desperately to preserve but find still-born.

□

Even a crossword puzzle is tacitly afraid of its own solution.

□

I must start to watch myself with the cunning persistence of a dog watching his fleas. This watching is delving deeply, noticing what is really significantly there. For the first time, understanding what has been all along. Does one have courage to do it? Is this what it means to be really alive, even if often scared and discouraged? Is this the last and maybe the most important opening into the meaning of myself and others? Is this the arduous path one must walk in order to become an integral being? A living instrument to help others to open a longing for enriched meaning through awareness. A servant to the one truth there is. A spokesman articulating haltingly the unknown, without a hope of deciphering it, since mystery grows through any attempt to understand it.

I must try to slow down my mind. Acceleration of any of its functions brings about a blurring, weakened attention, a sort of panoramic, general vision of reality. Mental speed reduces clarity and leads to a superficial observation of everything. The speedier my mind is, the less able am I to grasp anything, in terms of a strong, honest involvement in reality.

The task is to become sensitive to the 'unimportant' as in this scene from yesterday. A little boy was walking by. A tiny, fresh face, light hair, dark eyes, somehow lost in his dreams. Then he suddenly kicked a stone in his way. Not an angry movement, just the motion of a high spirit. And then he smiled. He had met a simple stone and had recognized its significance among things.

My mind slowed down with undivided attention and with a strange gratitude. That was the beginning of my awareness, followed by a feeling of gentle benediction.

□

Everything has an unknown side: a stone on the road, a passing cloud, human kindness and my mind also. That unknown side I will never know directly, but some fragment of it I may *understand* through the centre of my Self.

Thus, understanding always involves a rare knowing *of,* as contrasted with an intellectual knowing *about.* Knowing *of* is capable of capturing some meaningfulness of the unknown which is invariably mysterious.

□

I wish we played more often on our mental 'stereo' the natural markings in stones, the waves of the grain in wood, the ethereal dome of the vanishing dandelion, the river-maps in leaves — instead of the infernal noise of brutally chaotic banality of the so-called music, polluting our helpless ears and driving us insanely to a graceless jerk, we embarrassingly call dancing.

I may need more reform than anyone else. Thus, painfully am I mobilizing some as yet little known resources, which I trust can change me. What then is the general strategy? Primarily to seek an inner reform rather than revolution which is a deceptive process.

Note that a revolution, although usually mighty in its soaring, has a natural tendency (through its own peculiar gravity) to return in a full circle to its original point of departure. Inner or outer revolutionary zeal is actually only a tendency to establish a new arrangement of hierarchies within the same order of things. The same egotistic enterprise under a new shingle. Reform, in its proper sense, is a transformation, a creative change indifferent to any changing hierarchy of power.

So I need inner reform and not revolution, since some revolutions I have been in, left me deeply disappointed and unchanged. I need an inner progress and not circular motion.

□

In examining myself, I try, with a certain desperation, to complete myself. To add something that I presumably miss and that abounds in some other people. This may actually be a simple envy.

One resents not so much that something is missing, but that someone has something he doesn't have. A self-poisoning attitude, indeed.

Contrary to that, a wise man has at least temporarily a feeling of completeness. He finds it hard to be really jealous because he has lost the feeling of missing anything. And how well-wishing to us he can be in a warm and genuine sincerity, to the point of annoying us since we don't have it.

A shrewd man can never really like a wise man. The wise man reminds him painfully of his own incompleteness, inadequacies and shrill egotism.

In some ways I am a procrastinator. There are moments when I cannot bring myself to start or finish anything because I ruminate too much on the relative importance of things. What matters to me is the problem of preference. I am willing to use my energy and time only on what I consider productive and meaningful. Thus I am constantly selecting and rejecting.

Even though I know that selectiveness is mostly dictated by my gratification-seeking, I continue resorting to an established technique of sorting and arranging life. I carve it as a Thanksgiving turkey with a blunt knife. There is in it not only a lack of wisdom but plain, ungrateful stupidity. Thus naturally, when I refuse some aspects of life, the result is a selective blindness, the tension of impatience and futile anger. My intolerance feeds on my resentment and my life becomes a piecemeal concoction of tasteless gratifications.

□

Even the wind can teach us. It blows with an eagerness to be already somewhere else, to take part in an everlasting play. And where the other things vanish and pass, it inexhaustingly reappears, passing through.

□

To understand something is to be free of its past history as preserved in our memory. To be understood fully, a thing must appear suddenly, without any anticipation, evaluation and comment. We should learn to notice things not only as being 'recognized' from the past, but primarily as the carriers of always new and genuine vitality that makes them uniquely significant.

The power of understanding is a revelation that something *is* – and not what has been already noticed about it, or how it has been described before. This is the way a lover looks and understands.

Some of us are afraid of our inner darkness, as Job was of his unhealing scabs; but Job eventually knew that he saw more deeply and clearly in the darkness of his mother's body, than after being born.

□

Letting go gently. Leaving behind all that used to appear so important to our lives. Leaving behind habitual enjoyments, entertainments, successes, interests and even boredom. Assuming a serene detachment, which is of an unusual character, namely ceasing to favour something over something else with a compassionate acceptance, even toward ourselves. How difficult, and yet what a magnificent achievement of inner strength and humility.

To become ageless, without any disturbing desire and yet, more than before, heavily leaning on the timeless. Turning away from our distracted listening, to listen without any judgement, as the grass does. Turning away from our daily shrewd looking, to stare without any commentary at the movement of a tree branch.

Learning the most eloquent and true message of a brook passing by and of a bird flying beyond the horizon. A message of diminished purpose and growing meaning.

□

Consider that there does not exist a state of 'no' in nature; only our language and thought formulates it. Thus our repressions originate in instructions imposed upon us by society, not by nature.

□

Trying to understand the stars, human happiness, children, dreams and an unfolding flower is similar to a mosquito trying to bite a steel rail. Futile and yet what a glory in this trying.

60

A free person is totally natural like the curving of the roots of a tree. His freedom lies primarily in a capacity for taking deep delight in the fact that he is. His character is committed to an ego-less and natural uniqueness; he is willing to assent to his own destiny, and to that of those he loves.

He is free as a moon reflected in a lake, knowing, that although his image is left on the surface of the water, his essence is somewhere else. He knows deeply that nothing evil can happen to him, and if it does, then it happened to his image on the water of life, but never to his essence which endures.

A free person is a profoundly spiritual and independent person.

□

When one day, suddenly, everything becomes radiantly clear to you, you will happily and gratefully stretch in the grass, your face turned down to the earth.

From the beginning of time, I have been promised a paradise with the Unknown. Now, the Unknown attracts me more than the paradise. But do I really understand what is what and who is who?

□

Spirituality is a recognition of a communion with wholeness, with the joy and freedom of being. There is no exclusive spiritual territory (like formalized church religion) but there is a spiritual intention and commitment that transcends any religious denomination. Spirituality goes beyond any religion but fully actualizes religiosity. In it we happily fail to recognize how far life has entered into us and how far we have entered into life, and that unknown interaction fills us with wonder and awe.

□

The Creator is everything but a child, since a child is the surest premonition of death. The Creator is everything but a child, even if He is the most dedicated and splendid playmaker in the sands of the universe.

□

Certain things do not matter. It does not matter to a dead man whether it rains from above or from another direction. It does not matter to a puppy whether you press it against your cheek or against your ribs. It does not matter to the egg whether it is broken by a stone or by your inquisitive knuckle. It does not matter to a clock whether it marks a high noon or a dark midnight.

Similarly, it does not matter to God whether you are in life or in death.

□

To know a rose from its roots is to know her as the Creator did on the first day of creation.

When you hear the sound of the butterfly's wings folding over a flower, you know that Mozart is listening with you.

□

We can learn a powerful lesson from the Eastern mind that has matured over millennia and has flourished in a consciousness both less anxiety-ridden and often much deeper than ours. This consciousness has in it none of the split and alienation; it matures not into a state of individual, separate ego but into a deepening experience of spirituality in which the awareness of a Self is linked to the whole universe and finds in this merger a bliss.

There, man experiences himself as a part of the flow of cosmic energy which grew him into an individual and keeps growing him until the moment of return to the totality of energies. Maritain and Nishida would call it a pure and direct experience of unity — which is the direct opposite to the starting point of Descartes and his ego-committed: 'Cogito, ergo sum.'

□

One can explain ideas, the growth of weeds, quadratic equations, eastern standard time, orbiting stars. But the child's sudden awareness of life's glory — for that there are no words.

□

The first and last lesson of cosmic geometry for all sages, saints and very ordinary persons has been and remains to understand 'the point of intersection of the timeless with time.'

Faith is an unconditional acceptance of a total order of being of which one is a part, however small. It is an unreserved opening of a trust in a truth that is of the utmost significance in life. Faith is a willing plunge into the unknown, while disregarding cautions and safety margins. Faith is a high degree of courage and the best quality of freedom.

Belief, on the the other hand, is a cautious acceptance of possibilities that agree with certain criteria in a search for security. Belief has difficulty in relating to the unknown, since it originates in learned patterns of psychological dependencies on something or someone that gives comfort and protection in fearful and frustrated living. Belief is conditional and afraid of risk. It is a socialized and watered-down aspect of any genuine religiosity.

Belief is of considerable importance to any organized church, but totally unimportant in spiritual life. Through faith, one plunges headlong into the Amazon river of the unknown. Through belief, one slowly descends into the guarded waters of a communal pool, wrapped in a life-preserver.

□

How often we talk, because we don't know what to say; how often we talk knowing what to say, but never saying it; how often we talk, saying things we never knew; how often we talk to escape from the chill of the ineffable.

□

An insect is itself. A cobweb is itself. My shoe, a bird, a pine tree, they are all themselves without any further prerogatives. For them, to be oneself is the majesty of fleeting individuation confidently awaiting to be transcended.

Why then does my 'myself' give me so many difficulties? Because man takes his individuality so damned seriously.

Even a spiritual person seeks a verification of his mind's involvements with the universe. But he knows that it is not to be found in a dialectical transaction involving the reduction of facts (Russell's 'atomic facts') into logical propositions and measurements, but in a direct grasp of the pure, unarticulated and inexplicable ground of direct experiencing, without the mediation of logical verbalization. He is joyously aware that spiritual experience is the most direct and practical grasp of the unity of the visible and invisible, of the phenomenal and mysteriously hidden.

☐

To be born again. Why not? Most likely.
The same again? Most unlikely, maybe even boring.
As a chinchilla? Very funny, but possible.
As a tree? Most flattering, but possible.
As His children? Most certainly.

☐

The Creator is the most splendid, magnificent and majestic joker. And not only that, He is simultaneously a joker, a joke and our enjoyment of it. If we miss the point of the divine joke, we are without faith and thus frightened of His absolute wit.

Thus how can we really account for our fear, despair, anxiety and chronic lack of humour?

☐

Man's realization of grace is his recognition of an interdependence between himself and the whole universe. The leaf remembers its own tree trunk.

Social cosmetics do not stick to human oddballs, who are considered to be socially unprofitable, embarrassing, and what is even more damaging, downright failures. Yet they are natural and genuine like St. Francis in a shopping centre; they are memorable in their incapacity for being bribed, spoiled, mentally crew-cut or influenced by our shrewdness.

They are lovely people because they care for the essential radiation of grace, although often in a most ungraceful fashion; in that they are irrepressibly funny, as every cousin of an angel is.

□

Religiosity and creativity have fundamentally the same roots. Their effort is to expand reality beyond the limits of ordinary consciousness through symbolic expression.

The genuinely creative person experiences a presence of transforming grace and grateful compatibility with the 'Ruach Adonai', a wholeness and indivisibility of divine energy itself.

□

When people are entering into prayer, they are aware of a transition; when they are in it, they forget that they are praying.

□

We find too much self-justification in people not convincing, and too little of it, impertinent. We rather enjoy the sight of a sinner about whom we can say one or two good words.

Thus at once we feel kind, superior and totally self-justified.

Any myth offers to our finite intellect some symbolic suggestions about the ineffable infinite. Observe that many Christians feel rather uneasy when certain 'events' such as, for example, the Resurrection or the Immaculate Conception are referred to as being myths. This uneasiness is not necessary.

Myth does not mean an illusory fiction. Instead, it is a creative way of speaking *of* reality which is ineffable. It is a process of forming an analogy about the absolute. It represents metaphorically the Infinite in a finite expression. In its analogical and metaphorical power, myth is one of the most potent vehicles of human intelligence, achieving the closest approximation to any final truth.

Accordingly, if we form in our minds any image of God, that image has a value only as a genuine myth – and not as a description of any concrete actuality. To create an image of the Absolute becomes a unique tool in our desire to come as close as possible to Its reality, but that does not mean that the created myth *is* a concrete actuality of an event, state or person. Thus, any Christian myth is a highly creative intimation of the ineffable, but rarely a statement of an historic fact or event. It is a creative approximation of unknowable Reality that transcends our comprehension.

□

A fissure runs through the life of each of us; the presence of grace helps to mend it, to allow us to feel united again. The miracle of a promise: a broken vessel can hold water again.

□

Absent-mindedness is an ordinary defensive reaction in the everyday profane part of our lives, but a cardinal sin in the sacred part of our lives.

I used to play the violin for my grieving grandfather and yet, strangely enough, he never praised my music. But one day he gave me a puppy.

□

Man often longs to outlast himself, like a sound emerging from enduring vibrations a long time after the instrument's strings have returned to immobility.

□

I seem to be receding very slowly from so many futile and useless things of this life. Somewhat less disturbed, and more fascinated by every minute which, from time to time, is a carrier of unknown beauty and serenity. Without much fear, grief and regret, walking the remaining distance, as one comes closer home, with an utmost confidence.

Where then is the infamous 'thorn' of aging and dying if both are bringing closer the home-coming and the friendliest encounter with the final reality of everything? Receding slowly from the periphery to the very centre of life.

□

The sun illuminates a long time before it is visible, and a long time after setting behind the horizon: a daily rehearsal for eternity, and as usual, everyone is invited to the preview.

□

A darkened window waits patiently during the night to be formed again by the entering light of the morning.

□

Fire and faith have a great affinity. Both consume down to the essential, transform, and usually ascend in a silent cloud.

On the whole, the modern world rejects monasticism. The reason given is that it is antisocial. Yet, after all, to live in a highly communal discipline is to live together in this world which is cherished for its grace, meaning, work and inner beauty. And that is not a wish to abandon it as empty and sinful.

Some of the most accomplished monastic traditions, like the Benedictines and Tibetan Buddhists, are fully and eloquently clear about their way of admiring and respecting this world in many of its essential aspects, including the social. The fact that Trappists dislike idle talk, Dominicans idle students, and Benedictines prefer to eat their frugal food in silence, does not really make them antisocial – but wisely weary of our ego's incessant boasting about its phony sociability.

□

Pure happiness is a fragment of an explosion lodged in our amazed heart – and in its wake, an awesome silence dominates everything.

□

Some of us carry the ice-cube of faith into the sanctuary of our soul, nervously preoccupied with the possibility that it might melt before we arrive.

□

Beware of jogging. The healthiest exercise is walking along the paths of your inner mind where you meet things as they were before the expulsion from paradise.

A moment of bliss is never caused by somebody or something we know, but is a lightning that has flashed in the master cell of our centre, our soul. Bliss does not belong to us. It has occurred as a sudden self-reflection through which we reach beyond ourselves. A blissful person is always close to death, although he survives it and lives in the understanding that in bliss he has found the other side of death. He decides to live in an ever-renewed memory of that understanding. In that decision originates a unique quality of spiritual patience: not to wait anymore for anything to happen since it is already here from eternity.

□

'Something unknown is doing we don't know what.' Angels at it again, I guess.

□

Today I know more than ever that my hands are deeper in my being than my ideas, opinions and trained feelings. Thus, I can imagine how Moses once sat in front of a burning bush which illuminated his folded hands, ready to pray and give benediction.

□

There are big holes gaping even in the smallest things, and only children notice them and play with them. We adults are afraid of them because the more we age, the more we see them absorbing our life until, one day, emptiness is all.

□

So little we know about the origin of night. Yet the moon dwells in an awesome meaning, like a bugle thrown away in a deafening silence after the battle.

When I entered for the last time the room in which my
grandfather died, he was not there anymore. But neither was
death.

□

With every person's death, the total cosmos has momentarily
resigned from or abandoned a particular and unique experiencing
of itself. Thus our life is cosmically self-explanatory. Each of us,
while living, has a capacity to call the universe into being, and the
universe in turn confirms us as being alive. In terms of the
quantum theory, every object or subject shares all its properties
mutually and indivisibly with the system with which it interacts.

□

How often yet we shall die a 'small' death, before the most
significant 'non-awakening' will come about.

71

Sometimes, when gathering flowers, you become suddenly aware that the first and the most important encounter with death is its fragrance.

□

Death is only the other half of you. Death does not rob you, just the opposite. It completes you, joins with you and gives you, at last, cosmic integrity. Thus your birth is actually a splitting, a cutting into two halves, while the completion occurs through death.

Sometimes, rarely, in pure moments of your life, you hear a gentle distant calling; there, the other half of you longs for its double.

□

Often I worry that in the most decisive instance of my final jump into the unknown, I will badly twist the ankle of my hope, and when the dark waters close over my head, I will suddenly know, just one second too late, that the great radiant light endures.

□

Will you have the same name after you die? For those who knew you while alive, no problem; but what about those who are going to know you in eternity?

Maybe we all have two names – one for the register and one for eternity.

□

The last fingerprint left behind when the universe has stopped doing us, dancing us and singing us, is our dead body.

Then we become nothing less than an infinite act, the dance itself, and an enduring song.

72

To be confronted with death is not to be acquainted with it. Thus the only realistic way is to be acquainted with my death during my lifetime. That is to notice its presence as often as possible as it looms behind the impermanency of all that surrounds me. To notice my death not as a point in the future but as a continuous happening that permeates my life. That is the radical reconciliation with my own death: not as a future fearful accident, but as a present inseparable portion of my passing.

Only when my death is felt as a part of my daily living, every second of it, can I become familiar with it and communicate with it. If it is otherwise, I must be always frightened of death as a once-in-the-life episode that cuts me once and for all. Thus the only 'victory' over death is discovering it in the roots of everyday life as an ever present condition of it, without which life would lose its depth, value and beauty.

Death is a ground without which the figure of my life would be indistinguishable.

□

The mind grows serene thoughts as the lakeshore grows bulrushes. In certain seasons more luxuriantly and again more slowly until the great merciful snowfall covers all.

□

When at last we are in our coffin, we have permanently lost our shadow.

Our griefs are moments of arrest and paralysis of the process of ordinary living. We become captives of a huge invasion of inertia that temporarily chokes all our capacities to respond. Memories of the deceased one burn mercilessly and painfully. Any satisfactory and convenient solutions are remote and unreal. We are strangely suspended without any benefit of resourcefulness and inventiveness. Clouds of disconnected and helpless thoughts are aimlessly swarming around the frozen centre of ourselves. Our usually proud and effective intellect realizes its own futility, inadequacy and hollow superficiality.

Yet precisely at that time, we are mysteriously open to a very significant transformation that could occur in our lives. Grief can lead unexpectedly to a restructuring of our inner centre of gravity and become of crucial importance to our existence. It urges us that inner suspense and silencing, and even morbid agitation, can signal a regeneration, a deautomatization of our previous grieving responses.

In a sense, grief can paralyze our egos to such an extent that a profound reform takes place. We may then emerge from our grief with a new quality of detachment so that the horizon widens, the previous numbness slowly changes to a deepened but more serene sensitivity. Life enters into a larger frame and becomes more precious than ever before.

Any grief that enhances such a maturation can become a potential benediction and can lead to a permanent transformation previously unattainable.

□

Every October is a defiant splash of yellow acid between the eyes of death.

74

There are Sundays of heaviness and nostalgia. Sundays of longing for the unforgettably lovely. Sundays, when the inner rain falls on our agitated souls, and when the maturing heart feels a dislocation of time and space, before the dawn of meaning. Sundays of aging people, whose hearts know the vanity of all things. The hearts which do not ask for much any more, but which do not want to taste yet the waters of the dark underground, while the fireplace is maliciously alive in the ending of the afternoon. They seem to know that every dying is premature, since nobody has died at the 'right' time; right time being one without beginning and end.

Yet dying on Sunday has its own consolation: it happens on a day when our soul may be most ready to celebrate its belonging to an immensely higher order. The order of a transformed death.

□

At the moment of death, we may be gently and wisely reminded that we had never been planned to be more than we were already, from the beginning: an unimaginable and inexhaustible possibility.

□

It may be that the most humble and vital celebration of life is our ready and unproblematic willingness to inhale. Notice that nobody has died while inhaling.

□

The clouds are the first ones to leave behind the cemetery and a newly buried man.

75

One of the central concepts of the Japanese mind and sensibility is the word 'mujo' (memento mori). Meaning all things must soon pass away.

To the Westerner, that sentiment signals a start of melancholy and sadness, while to the Oriental, 'mujo' means that any attachment to anything is unwise. In this sense, the idea of death loses its sting, for death is everpresent and unavoidable.

The concept of 'mujo' is linked with the energy of human spirituality. As it avoids being constantly preoccupied with losing something, it concentrates on a radical awareness that with death a new cycle of being begins, even if temporary individual existence stops. 'Mujo' is the point of entry into Being without the burden of frustrating becoming. The resulting feeling is that of liberation in which one rejoices instead of fearing anything.

Every civilization centering on a similar interpretation of death is admirably capable of experiencing life's unending meaningfulness and beauty. For that reason, the Renaissance, for example, with its somewhat shrill preoccupation with life, finds despair in contact with death. On the contrary, Gothic transcendentalism, Dante for example, has a deeper vitality and robustness just because of its everpresent 'mujo'.

□

Everything is only once – and if it is twice, it is not the same anyway. Everything is mortal, even death, because it ends, where eternity begins.

76

Death relates to our being as a branch relates to a tree trunk; it is a running out of branching. Our temporal existence has run out, with it our ego, but not so our Self, which while being our innermost centre, is also shared by the whole universe.

Death is really not a private or personal happening but a universal re-channelling of constantly flowing and changing energy. When dying, our personal existence is threatened; when death takes place, no individual existence matters any more. Something stops growing and the branching is relocated.

□

Even the dead ones down in the earth know that we long for them. Through the hole left after the extracted violet, they see our faces turning away from daily twilight toward the gravity of amazing darkness.

□

A Requiem is a commentary on a mystery of receding waters that are slowly revealing the territory which we don't know now but from which we came.

□

One who at last enters the antechamber of death, will see all imaginary walls of reality recede into the void.

One who at last enters the antechamber of death, will forget himself while suddenly understanding that the endless endures.

One who at last enters the antechamber of death, will know the unknown which is not death.

ABOUT THE AUTHOR

Born in Czechoslovakia in 1922, Jaroslav Havelka acquired his
early university education during the German occupation of his
native country. After the war, he completed graduate work and
his Ph.D. at the University of Milan, Italy. There he studied
Psychology, Philosophy, and Comparative Literature.

When he came to Canada in 1952, he lectured in Slavic
literatures and Psychology of Literature at the University of
Montreal and completed an M.Sc. programme there in 1957.
During that time, while doing psychological research at McGill
University, he was awarded, in 1956, the First Prize for Literature
by the Slavonic-Christian Academy in Rome for his novella
Pelynek.

In 1957, he became an instructor in Psychology at The
University of Western Ontario and, in 1969, Professor and
Chairman of the Psychology department at King's College
(U.W.O.).

The author's major work is *The Nature of the Creative Process in
Art: A Psychological Study* (M. Nijhoff, The Hague, Holland,
1968). He was also selected to contribute to a book entitled
Teaching in The Universities: No One Way (McGill-Queen's
University Press, Montreal, 1974). His scholarly orientation cuts
across a number of disciplines but concentrates mainly on
Psychology of Personality, Cognitive and Creative functions,
Humanistic Psychology, and Eastern Psychology.

He helped to establish a Creativity Centre, in 1974, at King's
College, London, Ontario, and he has been consistently involved
in the centre's programmes which are designed for the
community at large.

In 1979, he published a book of psycho-philosophical essays (in
Czech) entitled *Breviar Podivovani* (Konfrontation, Zurich,
Switzerland).

His talents as a painter are also appreciated by many private
collectors in Canada and the United States.

For a number of years, his students and colleagues alike have
recognized Havelka as an excellent and inspiring teacher.